The
Taos Society
of Artists

MASTERS & MASTERWORKS

The Taos Society of Artists: Masters & Masterworks
Gerald Peters Gallery
1011 Paseo de Peralta
Santa Fe, New Mexico 87501

ISBN : 0-935037-78-0

Compiled by: Amy Scott
Text by: Amy Scott
Design: Laura McCurdy
Photography: Dan Morse
Printing: Advanced Litho, Inc., Great Falls, MT

Cover: Victor Higgins, *Aspens at Twining*, oil on canvas, 34 x 36 inches.

The
Taos Society
of Artists

MASTERS & MASTERWORKS

Table of Contents

During my twenty-five year career as a collector and dealer of western art, one of my primary goals has been to further research and scholarship on the Taos Society of Artists. Although its members were neither philosophically nor stylistically bound, together they produced a collective œuvre that remains as riveting and emotionally powerful today as it was during their heyday in the early 1920s. Their common goal to link Taos, an exotic and remote locale in turn-of-the-century America, indelibly with mainstream aesthetics was as unique as it was effective. Thus it was primarily through the Taos Society of Artists that America began its longstanding romance with the Southwest, which continues to this day.

In recent years, the Taos Society of Artists has been the focus of increasing attention from curators, collectors, scholars, and dealers. The result has been a gradual shift in the intellectual framework surrounding these artists, and they are now perceived less as academic regionalists than as pioneering founders of Taos' modern artistic legacy. Their responses to and interpretations of the region ranged from documentary to mythological in nature, resulting in a legacy steeped both in historic fact and romantic fiction. I have always found this combination compelling, and I hope that this carefully selected collection of works can be appreciated within this context.

Often referred to as the "Taos Ten," this publication seeks to redefine this extraordinary ensemble as the "Taos Twelve," with the inclusion of Julius Rolshoven and Catharine Critcher. Rolshoven and Critcher both enjoyed active membership status and participated in annual meetings and the exhibition circuit, but were not included in two consequential and now infamous photographs of their better known colleagues (staged after the Society disbanded, and Rolshoven and Critcher had returned to their careers in Italy and Washington D.C., respectively). Their absence, together with the fact that neither Rolshoven nor Critcher became full time residents of Taos, has resulted in an unfortunate neglect of their notable contributions. By reasserting their status as active and thus equal members of the Taos Society of Artists, our understanding and appreciation of the group can only be expanded.

This publication would not have been possible without the hard work and dedication of the Gerald Peters Gallery staff. My special thanks go to Amy Scott for contributing the text and coordinating the production of this catalogue, to our photographer Dan Morse for his sensitivity to the graphic presentation of the collection, and to Laura McCurdy for her design skills and attention to the printing details. I would also like to acknowledge the photographic archives at the Palace of the Governors, for granting reproduction rights for many of the documentary photographs utilized throughout this catalogue. Although the collection presented here is far from comprehensive, I hope that it will convey the depth and range of the artists and their work, and increase our understanding of both the individuals who comprised the Taos Society of Artists and the group as a whole.

Gerald P. Peters III

The Taos Society of Artists

When their wagon broke a wheel outside of Taos, New Mexico during a sketching trip from Denver to Mexico in September of 1898, neither Ernest Blumenschein nor Bert Phillips could have imagined the far-flung consequences of this seemingly unfortunate accident. After losing a coin toss to Phillips, Blumenschein began the twenty mile trek into Taos (where the nearest blacksmith was located), awkwardly balancing the broken wheel on his reluctant horse. As difficult and arduous as this journey was, it was also an artistic watershed for the young painter, an event that would change his life forever. Blumenschein's recollection of the experience reflects the impact that New Mexico had upon him:

> No artist had ever recorded the superb New Mexico I was now seeing. No writer had ever written down the smell of this air, or the feel of that morning's sky. I was receiving under rather painful circumstances, the first great unforgettable inspiration of my life. My destiny was being decided as I squirmed and cursed while urging the bronco through those many miles of waves of sagebrush . . . The sky was a clear, clean blue, with sharp, moving clouds. The color, the effective character of the landscape, the drama of the vast spaces, the superb beauty and serenity of the hills, stirred me deeply.

> I realized I was getting my own impressions from nature, seeing it for the first time with my own eyes, uninfluenced by the art of any man. Notwithstanding the painful handicap of that broken wheel I was carrying, New Mexico inspired me to a profound degree.

> My grunting horse carried me down and across the gorges, around the foothills over long flat spaces that were like great lakes of sage-brush, through twenty slow miles of thrilling sensations. It had to end in the Taos Valley, green with trees and fields of alfalfa, populated by dark-skinned people who greeted me pleasantly. There I saw my first Taos Indians, picturesque, colorful, dressed in blankets artistically draped. New Mexico had gripped me - and I was not long in deciding that if Phillips would agree with me, if he felt as inspired to work as I, the Taos valley and its surrounding magnificent country would be the end of our wagon trip. Mexico and other lands unknown could wait until the future.[1]

Not only did Phillips agree to stay and work with his friend, but within three months of their arrival he had made Taos his permanent home. Although Blumenschein later claimed that "none of us went there to found a colony, it just grew," the Taos Society of Artists became the first artists' group to create a signifi-

THE ACCIDENT THAT STARTED THE TAOS ART COLONY (BLUMENSCHEIN AND THE BROKEN WAGON, SEPTEMBER, 1898), (DETAIL).
PHOTO BY BERT PHILLIPS, COURTESY THE MUSEUM OF NEW MEXICO, NEG. NO. 40377.

cant body of work based on the landscape of northern New Mexico and the local Pueblo Indian culture. From the idyllic romanticism of Phillips and Eanger Irving Couse to the cubist experiments of Victor Higgins, the Taos Society of Artists was a collection of diverse individuals, in terms of both artistic style and personal character. Yet as a group they were highly organized and aggressively self-promotional. Their success was immediate, and as a result the Taos Society of Artists became the means through which both the members and Taos itself rose to national prominence.

The prehistory of the Taos Society of Artists (hereinafter referred to as the Taos Society or the Society) can be traced to Phillips and Blumenschein's encounter with Joseph Henry Sharp in 1895, while all three were studying at the Académie Julian in Paris. Sharp had visited Taos two years earlier on assignment for *Harper's Weekly*, and while in Paris regaled the younger artists with his vivid recollections of the region. When Phillips and Blumenschein journeyed to the area in 1898, they joined Sharp in his enthusiasm for Taos. After his return to New York (some three months later), Blumenschein maintained an active correspondence with Phillips, who had become an outgoing host for visiting artists. Motivated by his passion for the region as well as his isolation, Phillips urged Blumenschein to recruit painters for what he hoped was a fledgling art colony: "For heavens sake tell people about what we have found! Send some artists out

THE SIX FOUNDING MEMBERS OF THE TAOS SOCIETY OF ARTISTS (LEFT TO RIGHT): BLUMENSCHEIN, BERNINGHAUS, COUSE, PHILLIPS, SHARP, AND DUNTON (SEATED). PHOTO COURTESY THE MUSEUM OF NEW MEXICO, NEG. NO. 28820.

here. There's a lifetime's work for twenty men. Anyhow, I'm lonesome."[2]

Phillips did not remain lonely for long. Oscar Berninghaus, a St. Louis illustrator hired by the Denver and Rio Grande Railroad to sketch New Mexico and Colorado, befriended Phillips upon his initial visit in 1899. Eanger Irving Couse most likely met Phillips, along with Blumenschein and Sharp, at the Académie Julian in 1896; he made his first visit to Taos in 1902, presumably on Blumenschein's advice.[3] In 1912, while teaching at the Art Students League in New York, Blumenschein likewise encouraged his student, Herbert Dunton, to visit Taos; Dunton settled in Taos permanently later that year. When these six men banded together in July of 1915 to form the Taos Society of Artists, Sharp, Phillips, and Dunton were permanent residents, while Blumenschein, Berninghaus, and Couse were regular summer visitors.

As the Taos Society grew slowly but steadily in both numbers and national recognition, more of its members began to settle permanently in Taos, bringing their families and dedicating themselves wholly to the Southwest. Whereas the Taos Society founders primarily received their training in New York and Paris, Walter Ufer, Victor Higgins, and E. Martin Hennings were associates from Chicago and the Royal Academy in Munich. Each of these artists made their first visits to Taos on the advice of Chicago mayor and art patron Carter Harrison. After his first visit in 1914, Ufer considered Taos his primary home, although he continued to advance his reputation by exhibiting extensively in Chicago. Within a year of his arrival in Taos (also in 1914), Higgins likewise became a permanent resident. In 1919, after considerable negotiations with his wife, Blumenschein settled in Taos; Hennings followed suit in 1921. Although he did not join the Taos Society until 1926, Kenneth Adams had become a permanent resident upon his arrival two years earlier. Berninghaus eventually moved to Taos in 1925, and Couse established residency in 1927, the same year the Society disbanded.

Not all of the Society's members chose to relocate, however. Julius Rolshoven lived in Taos for approximately five years during World War I, before returning to Italy - his primary home for most of his life - around 1920. Catharine Critcher likewise did not stay; she summered in New Mexico during the 1920s, returning

BLUMENSCHEIN, PHILLIPS, SHARP, AND COUSE AT COUSE'S RESIDENCE.
PHOTO COURTESY THE MUSEUM OF NEW MEXICO, NEG. NO. 40386.

DUNTON OUTSIDE OF TAOS, CA. 1914-1916.
PHOTO COURTESY THE MUSEUM OF NEW MEXICO, NEG. NO. 116597.

to her successful career in Washington, D.C. each winter, where her portraits of the local Pueblo Indians received widespread acclaim. That Rolshoven and Critcher never established residency in Taos helps explain why they are all too often overlooked in literature on the Taos Society, despite the fact that they both enjoyed active membership status and successful careers in New Mexico as well as Italy and Washington, respectively.

While they were not the first to paint New Mexico (John Mix Stanley had visited the area as early as 1846; Worthington Whittredge worked in Santa Fe and Taos in the mid 1860s, and Thomas Moran painted the Northern Pueblos in the 1880s), the Taos Society members were responsible for establishing a national reputation for the region. Although the Society's growth in membership was gradual, its rise to national prominence has been described as meteoric. How was this phenomenal success achieved in such a relatively short period of time? From its inception, the Society established for itself a set of guidelines by which it closely controlled its membership, in terms of both the caliber of artists asked to join and the subjects they painted. At the Society's first meeting, the six founders decided that future nominees for membership must have worked in Taos for at least three years or part of three years and were required to have participated in a juried, representative American exhibition. In 1917 the Society decided members would be allowed to show only southwestern subjects in the annual exhibition circuit. The bylaws were further amended in 1919 to state that all members had to be American citizens. Together, these measures ensured an appropriate degree of aesthetic and thematic hegemony to the annual exhibition circuit, and that all members were

SHARP, PHILLIPS, COUSE, AND DUNTON IN TAOS (DETAIL), CA. 1914-1916. PHOTO COURTESY THE MUSEUM OF NEW MEXICO, NEG. NO. 116763.

MEMBERS OF THE TAOS SOCIETY OF ARTISTS. STANDING, LEFT TO RIGHT: **UFER, DUNTON. HIGGINS, ADAMS.** SEATED, LEFT TO RIGHT: **SHARP, HENNINGS, COUSE, BERNINGHAUS.** SEATED, FOREGROUND: **PHILLIPS** (LEFT), **BLUMENSCHEIN** (RIGHT).

focusing on the regional landscape and culture as they worked towards the common goal of creating a distinctly "American" art. The group also established a class of associate members - artists who exhibited with the Society, thus boosting the audience for and sales potential of the annual exhibition circuit. To this group they added nationally distinguished painters such as Robert Henri, John Sloan, and Randall Davey.

The Society's most prominent means of attracting attention was the annual exhibition circuit itself. Organized by the Society's secretary, the circuit traveled coast to coast each year, visiting urban venues such as New York, Boston, Cleveland, Nashville, Chicago, St. Louis, Kansas City, Denver, Salt Lake City, Los Angeles, and San Francisco.[4] The circuit was further promoted through an aggressive advertising campaign with considerable results. In the secretary and treasurer's report from 1917, Phillips wrote: "Our pictures have met with no little appreciation from thousands of people and a great deal of advertising matter has been printed and circulated until it would be difficult to find a person in the whole country making any pretension to being posted in art matters who has not heard of Taos and the 'Taos Society of Artists.'"[5] By 1921 the Taos Society had accumulated enough national prestige to claim a Fifth Avenue (New York City) venue, The Kingore Gallery. The exhibition was extremely well received - a "very great success among the people there. . . the newspapers of New York City, even the magazines, took up [the] exhibition and did it great justice."[6]

The pioneering status, productive beginning, and subsequent reputation enjoyed by the Taos Society have obscured the fact that it was not always the well-oiled sales and exhibition machine it is often assumed to have been. There is evidence of trouble between members as early as 1918, following Blumenschein's attempt to lead the group in painting "Range Finders," or large scale European landscapes to be used in military camps for training soldiers to estimate distance and strategic points.[7] Apparently, he was somewhat disappointed with their efforts. After Blumenschein published a letter "which reflected most unpleasantly on the patriotism and attitude of [the] members, towards their activity in war work"[8] in the September 14 issue of *American Art News*, he was quick to issue an apologetic response. Later tiffs were not so easily amended, however. In 1922, Dunton became the first member to resign. Although the exact circumstances surrounding his decision remain unclear, it was most likely due to his unwillingness to serve as secretary (The Society had a policy of rotating members through the offices alphabetically), a task which had become a cumbersome and thankless one. A letter from Blumenschein to Berninghaus, dated July 15, 1922, further suggests that Dunton resigned for personal reasons, and that certain members were beginning to get on one another's nerves: "Mr. Dunton told Couse that his reason for resigning was because he did not care to belong to a society in which the sec'y [Ufer] referred to the president [Blumenschein] as a 'bald-headed S. B.'" Blumenschein himself left the following year, claiming he could not serve as secretary due to his obligations in another group he had helped form (The New Mexico Painters). After a heated debate during which Ufer stormed out of the room (forcing Berninghaus to act as chairman in his stead), the Society rejected Blumenschein's excuse, and he subsequently resigned.[9]

DUNTON (LEFT) AND BERNINGHAUS ON HORSEBACK OUTSIDE OF TAOS, C. 1914-1916.
PHOTO COURTESY THE MUSEUM OF NEW MEXICO, NEG. NO. 116649.

Sales from the annual exhibition circuit were also suffering by 1923. That year, critics of the circuit began to complain that the prices were too high, and that the works in general were more commercial than reflective of the artists' true talents. Poor sales may have been the reason behind the election of Hennings and Critcher to active membership in 1924 (by which time Dunton and Blumenschein had already resigned). Indeed, immediately following their election, sales were reported as "encouraging," and the exhibition circuit to be "stronger and better than ever." Regardless, the 1925 circuit continued to be plagued by complaints of high prices, and at the 1926 annual meeting "Principal discussion was in regard to placing future exhibitions where at least one sale would be made."[10]

The Taos Society disbanded in 1927, at a meeting which was not recorded. Kenneth Adams later wrote in the *New Mexico Quarterly* (Summer 1951) that "a quorum of [Taos Society] members met at the home of Bert G. Phillips one night in March, 1927, and by a unanimous vote ended the existence of the Taos Society of Artists." The suggestion that the Society ended over discord between members and lagging sales neither diminishes nor obscures its numerous accomplishments. Despite its unceremonious end, the Taos Society of Artists introduced a nation to the landscape and Indian culture of northern New Mexico, a popular fascination that continues to this day. It was further responsible for helping establish Taos as a significant twentieth century artists' colony which later attracted some of America's premier modernists, including Georgia O'Keeffe, John Marin, Stuart Davis, and Marsden Hartley. Other groups attempted to follow in its footsteps, such as the New Mexico Painters (founded in 1923 by Blumenschein, Ufer, Higgins, B.J.O. Nordfeldt, William P. Henderson, Gustave Baumann, Jozef Bakos, and Frank Applegate) and the Taos Artists Association (founded by Sharp, Blumenschein, Berninghaus, Leon Gaspard, Joseph Fleck, and Andrew Dasburg), but none enjoyed the same degree of national notoriety and influence as the Taos Society of Artists. As Berninghaus aptly stated, during its heyday the Taos Society was "undoubtedly one of the best known [artists' groups] in the United States."[11]

Amy Scott
Curator, Gerald Peters Gallery

TAOS MOUNTAINS (DETAIL), CA. 1914-1916. PHOTO COURTESY THE MUSEUM OF NEW MEXICO, NEG. NO. 116602.

The Artists

Joseph Henry Sharp is often referred to as the most beloved member of the Taos Society, a reference to both his fatherly role within the group and his benevolent reputation around town. Sharp's tightly painted and strictly composed scenes were strongly influenced by his extensive European training, and the popularity he enjoyed throughout his career was based in part on his reputation as a faithful portrayer of Indian life.

Born in Bridgeport, Ohio in 1859, Sharp went to work in a nail factory at the age of twelve or thirteen in order to help support his family. Within two years he moved to Cincinnati, where he briefly studied at the McMicken School of Design before entering the Cincinnati Art Academy. After nearly ten years of training in the Cincinnati area, Sharp left for Europe in 1881, studying in Antwerp and Belgium for a year. After his return to the U.S., he made his first of many journeys west in 1883, visiting Santa Fe, Arizona, California, and Wyoming, where he sketched several of the local Indian tribes. By 1886 he had resumed his studies in Europe at the Royal Academy in Munich, with Frank Duveneck in Italy, and at the Académie Julian in Paris. In 1892 he returned to Cincinnati, where he supported himself by teaching at the Art Academy and painting commissioned portraits of local society members. Sharp made his second trip west in 1893, when he visited Taos for the first time. Thrilled with the mountain landscape and fascinated by the Indian culture, he enthusiastically related his impressions of Taos to his younger colleagues Ernest Blumenschein and Bert Phillips, whom he met upon his subsequent return to the Académie Julian the following year.

Having secured considerable academic credentials, Sharp returned again to Cincinnati in 1897, where he taught for several years before establishing residency in Crow Agency, Montana in 1902. There his respect for the Indians' intrinsic connection to their surroundings, ancestral history, and customs was intensified by what he saw as the gradual destruction of a timeless culture by encroaching Anglo civilization. Inspired by his genuine affection and regard for the Indians, Sharp spent the next several years chronicling the appearance and traditions of several of the Plains tribes, including the Crow, Sioux, Dakota, and Nez-Percè. His honest depictions of his Indian subjects as the proud, rightful inhabitants of their dwindling lands were popular with Eastern collectors and museums. Indeed, the Smithsonian Institution purchased several works primarily on their value as ethnographic documents.

In 1912, Sharp moved permanently to Taos, partly because of the decline of traditional Plains Indian culture but also due to the increasing availability of native models in New Mexico. Sharp's enthusiasm and easy familiarity won the favor of his Indian models, several of whom became his close friends. He was also admired and well-liked by his fellow members of the Taos Society of Artists, which he helped found in 1915. Next to Julius Rolshoven, Sharp was the senior and most experienced member of the Society. He was also among the more active; he continued to travel throughout his career, visiting Europe, Hawaii, Japan, and Latin America. Despite the delight he found in the new, Sharp remained committed to academic principles he acquired during his extended studies in Europe. The resulting reputation he enjoyed can be seen as evidence of the degree to which academic doctrine persisted as a legitimate means of expression in American painting long after the turn of the century.

15

Other Medicine, Crow, oil on canvas, 18 x 12 inches.

War Bonnet Maker, oil on canvas, 20 x 24 inches.

Rio Grande, oil on canvas, 12 1/8 x 18 1/8 inches.

Sunlight and Shadows, oil on canvas, 21 x 31 1/2 inches.

John and Jerry (Hunting Son and Elkfoot), oil on canvas, 22 3/8 x 21 inches.

Prince of Peace, oil on canvas, 14 x 10 inches.

Bear Goes to the Otter Ground, Crow, oil on canvas, 16 x 12 inches.

Moonlight, Taos Pueblo, oil on canvas, 16 x 20 inches.

Montana Landscape, oil on canvas, 16 1/8 x 24 1/4 inches.

Persian Lilacs and Chinese Embroidered Background, oil on canvas, 24 1/4 x 36 inches.

Bert Phillips' penchant for rural, pastoral settings can be traced to his earliest known paintings, executed during his student days in New York. While studying in Europe he gravitated towards the Barbizon School, which emphasized the morality believed to be inherent in an agrarian lifestyle. These tendencies carried over to Phillips' work in Taos as well. Painted in traditional dress and shown relaxing, dancing, or engaged in ritual, Phillips' Indians lead a romantic, ideal existence untouched by time or Anglo civilization.

Bert Phillips was born in the industrial town of Hudson, New York in 1868. He later recalled of his childhood that he could always be found with a brush in hand, and when George McKinstry opened an art studio in Hudson around 1884, Phillips was among the first to enroll. Other early influences on Phillips were the tales of Indians and western adventure found in James Fenimore Cooper's *Leatherstocking Tales* and the exploits of the famous Indian agent Kit Carson. At the age of sixteen, Phillips left home for New York City, where he studied at the Art Students League and the National Academy of Design before leaving for England in 1894. From London he soon went to Paris to study at the Académie Julian, where he befriended Ernest Blumenschein and Joseph Henry Sharp. After his return to New York in 1896, he rented a studio with Blumenschein, who convinced Phillips to accompany him on a journey west in the Spring of 1898. From New York the artists made their way to Denver, where they outfitted themselves with horses, a wagon, camping and art supplies, and with a large Navy revolver, headed for Mexico. When they broke a wagon wheel on the rough terrain of northern New Mexico, Phillips waited with their equipment while Blumenschein set out on horseback to have the wheel repaired in nearby Taos. Blumenschein returned three days later, and the two continued on to Taos, where they sold their wagon, harness, and remaining horse, and "pitched into work with unknown enthusiasm."[1] Although Blumenschein returned to New York within three months, Phillips decided to stay permanently.

Phillips was intrigued by the rough, border town history of Taos, the home of his boyhood hero Kit Carson and the site of legendary conflicts such as the Taos rebellion and massacre of 1847. Phillips' ambition to live the western adventures he had read about might have been among the causes of a skirmish that ensued after he and a friend refused to remove their hats during a religious ceremony on the plaza. The incident resulted in the death of the sheriff and increased tension between the Anglo and Hispanic residents of Taos. Phillips, however, was excited by the dangerous turn of events, as he enthusiastically related in a letter to Blumenschein: "I began to feel as if this was real 'border life,' and only wish old Kit Carson was here with us."[2]

In addition to real adventure, Phillips found an unlimited source of subject matter in the mountain landscape and colorful Indian culture that surrounded him in Taos. In 1899 he married Rose Martin, the sister of the local doctor, and began corresponding with Blumenschein in New York about forming an art colony. Always willing to make arrangements for visiting artists, Phillips played an instrumental role in the growth of Taos as an artistic center, and was a founding member of the Taos Society of Artists in 1915. His taste for drama may have also been the source of the romantic, poetic nature of much of his art. To Phillips, who spent more years in the town than any other member of the Taos Society, Taos was a place where "a distinctive American art idea should develop on a soil so imbued with romance, history, and scenic beauty."

Song of the Flute, oil on canvas, 20 x 24 inches.

The Water Carrier, oil on canvas, 20 x 14 inches.

After the Ceremony, oil on academy board, 24 3/8 x 75 1/2 inches.

The Rabbit Hunter, oil on canvas, 9 3/4 x 7 3/4 inches.

Untitled (Taos Lane in Spring), oil on canvas, 13 x 17 inches.

Autumn Rhythm, oil on masonite, 12 3/8 x 11 1/2 inches.

Outspoken Taos Society of Artists founder Ernest Blumenschein was a colorful and sometimes controversial figure whose character was marked by boundless energy and fierce determination. A staunch supporter of Post-Impressionism, Blumenschein's own style is marked by the use of deep, rich colors and a strict sense of spatial geometry and rhythm. Possibly the most complex and least understood member of the Taos Society, Blumenschein's southwestern pictures were often born of the artist's interest in formal integrity and harmony rather than a desire to accurately portray Pueblo culture.

Similar to several of his later Taos colleagues, Blumenschein was of modest, midwestern beginnings. Born on May 26, 1874 in Pittsburgh, Pennsylvania, Blumenschein moved to Dayton, Ohio in 1878, following the death of his mother. Encouraged by his father (who was the director of the Dayton Philharmonic), Blumenschein earned a scholarship to study at the Cincinnati College of Music upon graduating from high school. After taking an illustration course from Fernand Lungren at the Cincinnati Art Academy, Blumenschein decided to pursue a career in the visual arts, and in 1892 he moved to New York to study at the Art Students League. He soon became convinced that European study was necessary in order to establish himself as a professional artist, and in 1894 he enrolled at the Académie Julian in Paris, where he became acquainted with Bert Phillips and Joseph Henry Sharp. Somewhat older and more experienced than Blumenschein or Phillips, Sharp regaled the younger artists with fantastic tales of his 1893 visit to Taos, New Mexico.

Upon his return from Paris in 1896, Blumenschein worked as an illustrator in New York, where he shared a studio with Phillips. After an assignment that took him to Arizona and New Mexico in the winter of 1898, Blumenschein persuaded Phillips to make another journey west with him that Spring. When a broken wagon wheel landed the artists in the nearby town of Taos, Phillips decided he had reached the end of his journey. Blumenschein stayed in Taos for three months, returning to his lucrative illustration career in New York, and eventually to Paris for further study at the Académie Julian, in 1899 and again from 1902 to 1909. During this latest and longest stay he met and married Mary Shepherd Greene, an established artist whose work was often featured in the prestigious annual Salon.

After their return to New York in 1909, the couple worked as an illustration team and Blumenschein began teaching at his alma mater, the Art Students League. He also started spending his summers in Taos in 1910, and settled there permanently in 1919. As a founding member of the Taos Society of Artists, Blumenschein was deeply involved with the group from its inception in 1915. In 1918 he led members in painting "Range Finders" - large scale European landscapes used to teach soldiers how to estimate distances and find strategic points. Blumenschein also served as president from 1920-1921, but refused the position of secretary in 1923, claiming that he was already committed to an office in another group he had helped form (The New Mexico Painters). After a heated debate the other members decided to reject his excuse, and Blumenschein subsequently resigned from the Society.

ERNEST L. BLUMENSCHEIN IN HIS STUDIO

Church at Chimayo, oil on canvas, 16 x 20 inches.

Indian Dance, oil on canvas, 24 x 27 inches.

Untitled (Mountain Wood Gatherers), oil on canvas, 23 x 50 inches.

Untitled (Nude with Drapery), oil on panel, 13 1/2 x 10 1/4 inches.

Untitled (Taos Landscape), oil on canvas, 20 x 16 inches.

Feast Day, Ranchos Church, Taos, oil on canvas, 25 x 30 inches.

A central figure of the Taos Society of Artists from its inception to its demise, Oscar Berninghaus was, unlike most of his colleagues in the group, a largely self-taught artist. Berninghaus used his powers of observation, primarily a result of his extensive background in illustration, to record his surroundings with journalistic accuracy. His diligence and attention to detail resulted in a realistic body of work that documents the changes Taos Pueblo culture underwent in the first quarter of the twentieth century as well as the picturesque appeal of the region and its inhabitants.

Born on October 2, 1874 in St. Louis, Missouri, Berninghaus developed an interest in watercolor as a child by observing his father's lithography business. During his time spent sketching the bustling Saint Louis riverfront, the young Berninghaus was fascinated by the wild tales of western adventure he heard from cowboys and trappers passing through. By the age of twelve, he was an accomplished watercolorist with a head for business, and often sold his sketches of local scenes to newspapers and tourists. In 1890 Berninghaus quit school in favor of a job with the lithography company Compton & Sons, where he acquired a technical knowledge of printmaking, engraving, and color separation. Three years later he joined the firm of Woodward and Tiernan, then one of the largest printing companies in the world. He also enrolled in night classes at Washington University and continued to paint and sketch in his spare time. Despite his lack of European training (unlike his contemporaries Blumenschein, Phillips, Couse, and Sharp, Berninghaus never studied in Paris), his work experience, together with his sense of self-discipline, instilled in him a lifelong respect for the academic principles of three-dimensional space, composition, and movement.

Due to his rapidly growing reputation, in 1899 Berninghaus was hired by the Denver and Rio Grande Railroad to sketch the landscape of Colorado and New Mexico for promotional purposes. Upon arriving in Taos, Berninghaus was captivated by the dominant Indian culture, as well as the austere landscape and the intense colors of the late afternoon light. He also befriended Bert Phillips, a permanent resident since his accidental arrival the previous year. Although Berninghaus initially spent only a week in Taos, he returned nearly every summer in subsequent years. These visits soon turned into six month stays, and he settled there permanently in 1925. For Berninghaus, Taos was a conduit for what he felt was a uniquely American expression: "We have had French, Dutch, Italian, and German art. Now we have American art. I feel that from Taos will come that art."[1]

One of the six founding members of the Taos Society of Artists, Berninghaus was present at the historic first meeting in July of 1915, where he was elected temporary chairman. Berninghaus' penchant for order and harmony, a chief quality of his work, also served the Society well. During its twelve year existence, Berninghaus spent more time in the difficult and painstaking office of secretary than any other member. Other contributions included his own national reputation, which added to the Society's prestige. His continued association with midwestern and eastern organizations, including the Society of Western Artists, the Salmagundi Club, and the National Academy of Design, made Berninghaus one of the more financially and critically successful members of the Taos Society of Artists.

OSCAR E. BERNINGHAUS

40

Apache Camp, Boulder Lake, watercolor, 15 3/4 x 19 3/4 inches.

Road Under Cottonwoods, oil on canvas, 30 x 36 inches.

Taos Visitors to the Chuck Camp on the Rio Grande Plateau, oil on canvas, 30 x 36 1/4 inches.

Indian Chief and Pony, oil on canvas, 25 x 30 inches.

Indians on the Mesa, oil on panel, 16 x 20 inches.

In Our Valley, oil on canvas, 20 x 24 inches.

Sage Brush in Bloom on the Mesa, oil on canvas, 24 1/4 x 28 inches.

Indian in White Robe, oil on board, 13 x 9 inches.

Horses Grazing in Taos Mountains, NM, oil on board, 12 x 9 7/8 inches.

Eanger Irving Couse's distinctive style and characteristic paintings of Indian subjects, often dramatically lit by twilight or romantic firelight, earned him an international reputation in the first quarter of the twentieth century. Commissioned for many years to supply pictures to the annual calendars of the Santa Fe Railway Company, Couse has long been acknowledged as one of the more nationally recognizable and commercially successful members of the Taos Society of Artists.

Born on September 3, 1866 in Saginaw, Michigan, Eanger Irving Couse was familiar with Indian daily life and rituals from an early age, earning a reputation (even as a boy) for his faithful depictions of the local Chippewa tribe. After raising tuition by painting houses in his home town, Couse traveled to Chicago and enrolled in the Art Institute in 1883. The following year he returned briefly to Michigan before moving to New York, where he enrolled in the prestigious National Academy of Design. By 1886 the twenty-one year old Couse was lured to Paris, then the cosmopolitan art center of the western world. He quickly enrolled in the Académie Julian, which attracted numerous Americans due to its reputation for tolerance when it came to experimentation. At Julian's (as it was known to its American contingent), Couse was profoundly influenced by his professor, William Adolphe Bouguereau, who preached a classical doctrine based on Renaissance techniques and Christian values. A devout Christian himself, Couse would never relinquish the principles he learned from Bouguereau, and adhered to French academic conventions throughout his career. Within a year of his arrival in Paris, Couse had one of his pictures accepted into the prestigious annual Salon, an event often equated with a professional coming of age for young artists. That year he also married Virginia Walker, a fellow American art student in Bouguereau's atelier for women.

Couse and his new wife lived briefly in Oregon in 1891, but quickly returned to the Académie Julian before moving to Normandy where he worked for three years, painting local fishing and pastoral scenes. By 1896 or 1897 he was back in Oregon, painting the peaceful lifestyle of several Northwest Indian tribes, including the Klickitat and Umatilla. Couse made his first trip to Taos in 1902, most likely on the advice of Ernest Blumenschein, his compatriot from Paris. By 1906, he had established a residence and studio in Taos, where he painted primarily during the summers, returning to New York each winter (no doubt many of Couse's paintings of Indian subjects were finished in his New York studio, consistent with French academic practice). In 1914 Couse's Indian paintings attracted the attention of William Simpson, the head of advertising for the Santa Fe Railway. Over the next two decades, his work would be featured twenty-three times in the railway's promotional calendar. The calendar's widespread circulation (it was featured in over 300,000 schools and businesses) made Couse one of the more prominent artists in the country.

A founding member of the Taos Society of Artists, Couse served as its first president. His leadership role continued throughout the lifespan of the Society; he was unanimously reelected president in 1918, serving until 1920. He also served as secretary in 1924, a cumbersome job that entailed organizing the annual exhibition circuit (indeed, the office of secretary was often viewed as a burden and some members were reluctant to serve, as was the case with Ernest Blumenschein and Herbert Dunton). Despite his heavy involvement with the Society, Couse did not move permanently to Taos until 1927, thereafter devoting himself entirely to painting the traditions, culture, and daily lives of the Pueblo Indians.

The Young Hunter oil on canvas, 38 x 81 1/2 inches.

White Prince, oil on canvas, 49 3/4 x 60 7/8 inches.

Pawhyumma Umitilla Indian, oil on canvas, 25 1/4 x 32 1/2 inches.

The Camping Place, oil on canvas, 24 x 29 inches.

Campfire in the Aspens, oil on canvas, 24 x 29 inches.

Evening at the Riverbank, oil on canvas, 30 x 36 inches.

Spirit in the Pool, oil on canvas, 29 3/8 x 24 3/8 inches.

Quiet Pool, oil on canvas, 29 1/4 x 24 1/8 inches.

Hunting for Deer, oil on canvas, 24 x 29 inches.

Standing Indian with Child, oil on canvas, 12 x 5 1/2 inches.

Moonlight on the Lake, oil on masonite, 12 x 15 7/8 inches.

61

The fame of Herbert "Buck" Dunton, the sixth founding member of the Taos Society of Artists, rests primarily on his reputation as a painter of the expansive plains of western cattle country.[1] Dunton's renditions of the open range helped perpetuate the myth of cowboy life as a rugged, isolated existence, even as the great cattle empires were dwindling in the face of a growing population geared more towards industry and commerce. Often dwarfed by the immense landscapes they inhabit, Dunton's lone cowboys and healthy game contributed to the popular notion of the American West as a land of both tranquil isolation and natural bounty.

Born on August 28, 1878 in Augusta, Maine, Dunton grew up on his great grandmother's farm in Newport, Rhode Island. As a child he spent his days drawing or hunting with "Gramps," and cared little for school, which he quit at age sixteen. After working odd jobs for two years Dunton left for Montana, where he worked as a cowboy, a meat supplier to ranches, and an assistant to a bear hunter. He also began a serious study of animal anatomy, from horses and cattle to large game. Despite his intrinsic dislike of cities, in 1903 Dunton moved to New York where he quickly established a reputation as an illustrator of western stories and articles, with commissions from national magazines such as *The Amateur Sportsman*, *Harper's Weekly*, and *The Saturday Evening Post*. (After the death of Frederic Remington in 1909, Dunton's fame as a chronicler of cowboy life was second only to that of Charles Russell, with whom he became good friends.) He also enrolled in classes at the Art Students League, where he heard of the mountain hamlet of Taos from his instructor, Ernest Blumenschein. Presumably on Blumenschein's advice, Dunton moved to Taos in 1912.[2]

The last founding member of the Taos Society to arrive, Dunton occupied a series of studios before buying a large house which he dubbed "La Solana" (the sunny place) in 1923. Like several of his colleagues, he was also a great outdoorsman and spent much of the year camping and hunting, often in the company of Blumenschein or Berninghaus. Dunton' s association with the Taos Society ended in 1922, when he became the first member to resign. Although the reasons behind his decision remain unclear, evidence suggests bad feelings were developing between members. A letter from Blumenschein to Berninghaus, dated July 15, 1922, states that "Mr. Dunton told Couse that his reason for resigning was because he did not care to belong to a society in which the Sec'y [Ufer] referred to the President [Blumenschein] as a 'bald-headed S.B.'" The minutes from the 1924 annual meeting, at which Dunton was briefly reconsidered for membership, suggest there was another reason behind his original resignation: his unwillingness to serve as secretary. Perhaps wishing to avoid a controversy similar to the one that surrounded Blumenschein's 1923 resignation (also over his unwillingness to serve as secretary), the Society decided it would be "inadvisable" to reelect Dunton to membership until "he would agree to fulfill what was considered a former obligation."[3]

The Cow Puncher, oil on canvas, 16 x 12 inches.

Noon Break, oil on canvas, 30 1/8 x 20 inches.

The Chief, oil on canvas, 20 x 16 inches.

The Open Range, oil on canvas, 26 x 39 inches.

Portrait of a Warrior, oil on canvas, 35 x 22 inches.

Evening on the Cattle Range, oil on canvas, 8 x 10 1/8 inches.

Among Walter Ufer's contributions to the Taos Society of Artists was a straightforward, tactile representation of Pueblo life and culture and his sensitivity to the tension inherent in the gradual absorption of one culture by another. Ufer was both a humanitarian and political radical whose belief in labor rights and security extended to artists. Academic in composition yet less romantic than those of Couse, Sharp, or Phillips, Ufer's Taos pictures were extremely popular with his Chicago patrons while presenting a more objective view of Pueblo life.

Born in Lexington, Kentucky in 1876, Walter Ufer was apprenticed to a local commercial lithographer after his father recognized his nascent talent for drawing. Ufer left Lexington (which he thought a "dull tobacco and whiskey town") for Germany in 1893, where he studied in Hamburg and at the Royal Academy of Fine Arts in Dresden. Although he was to make several more excursions to Germany over the next twenty years, Ufer settled in Chicago in 1900, the cosmopolitan outlet of the midwest. There he earned a living by working in advertising and teaching art at the J. Francis Smith School. In 1911 Ufer returned to Germany for two years of further study at the Royal Academy in Munich, where he worked alongside Victor Higgins and Martin Hennings, both fellow artists from Chicago.

Ufer returned again to Chicago in 1913, where he initially struggled to make his way as a professional artist. Fortunately, his work soon attracted the attention of Carter Harrison, then serving his fifth term as mayor. Harrison bought two works at Ufer's first one man sale and encouraged the artist to visit New Mexico. Towards the end of the summer of 1914, Ufer left for Taos, where he became acquainted with Buck Dunton, Bert Phillips, and Joseph Sharp. During this visit Ufer also gained the patronage of Oscar Mayer and Charles Herrmann, both of whom would become important collectors of his work. Although he returned to Chicago within a few months, he began actively corresponding with his new associates and spending part of each year in Taos. The following summer he brought his wife, Mary, with him, and as his time spent in New Mexico increased, so did his associations with the Taos Society members. In August of 1916, he was invited to show with the Taos Society in a Santa Fe exhibition, and at the annual meeting on July 15, 1917, he was elected to active membership along with Victor Higgins. A member until the Society's demise in 1927, Ufer was strongly associated with the group and painted southwestern subjects almost exclusively during the 1920s.

Ufer's ability to capture the dazzling New Mexican sunlight resulted in a dramatic use of shadow and lively, patterned surfaces. Unlike most of his colleagues, Ufer was uninterested in romanticizing Pueblo life to correspond with the picturesque landscape. As they stoically succumb to the pressures of modernization without enjoying the benefits, Ufer's Indian subjects often allude to the difficult transition Pueblo culture underwent during the early twentieth century.

June Storm, oil on canvas, 25 1/4 x 30 1/4 inches.

Coming from the Spring, oil on canvas, 25 3/8 x 30 1/2 inches.

Indian Corn Field, San Juan, NM, oil on artist board, 10 3/4 x 12 1/8 inches.

A December Day, oil on canvas, 20 x 20 inches.

The Desert Trail, oil on canvas, 20 x 25 inches.

Victor Higgins was perhaps the most stylistically flexible and experimental member of the Taos Society. During his lengthy and prolific career he worked in a variety of stylistic idioms, from his early impressionist works to the later cubist landscapes. From the time of his first visit to Taos in 1914, Higgins' work reflects an interest in the relationship between geometric forms as a means of conveying space and constructing composition. Characterized by scholars as a gentleman who painted in a three-piece suit, Higgins was a business minded intellectual whose work reflects a consuming interest in the creation of a distinctly American art.

Born in Shelbyville, Indiana on June 28, 1884, Victor Higgins grew up on a small midwestern farm. As a child, his interest in art was sparked by a traveling sign painter, and at the age of fifteen he left home for Chicago, where he studied for the next ten years at the Art Institute and the Chicago Academy of Fine Art. After a brief trip to California, Higgins traveled to New York in 1911 where he met Robert Henri and George Bellows, members of the "Ashcan School," who advocated painting from experience for an honest representation of everyday American life. Higgins left for Europe later that year, spending time in England and Paris as well as Munich, where he worked with Martin Hennings and Walter Ufer. In 1913 he returned to Chicago in time to view the breakthrough Armory show, which had traveled from New York in a reduced format. As it traced the development of modernism from Manet to Picasso, the Armory show introduced Higgins to the work of leading European and American modernists, including John Marin, who was applying cubist principles to his paintings of the American landscape.

Prompted by Chicago mayor and art patron Carter Harrison, Higgins made his first visit to Taos in 1914, and established residency the following year. In Taos, the seemingly unchanged lifestyle of the Pueblo Indian provided a key subject which Higgins used to express his belief in the dignity inherent in a lifestyle of modesty and self-reliance. In 1915 Higgins received his first one man show in Santa Fe, and in 1917 he was invited to join the Taos Society of Artists along with Walter Ufer (with whom he had become close friends). Although Higgins attended most meetings between his induction and the time the Society disbanded in 1927, there is little evidence to suggest he was an exceptionally involved or devoted participant. By 1920, rather, Higgins had begun a slow separation from the Taos Society, spending more time with the progressive Andrew Dasburg and his student Kenneth Adams.

After the Taos Society disbanded in 1927, Higgins increased his forays into Cubism. When John Marin, a member of Alfred Stieglitz's avant-garde circle in New York, arrived in Taos in 1929, Higgins began to concentrate more fully on pattern, working primarily in watercolors. While the extent of Marin's influence on Higgins remains unclear, the increasingly abstract nature of his work in the late 1920s and 30s suggests a profound encounter with something new, as well as a logical continuation of his lifelong interest in experimentation.

Landscape, watercolor, 13 3/4 x 19 3/4 inches.

Autumnal Landscape, oil on canvas, 16 1/4 x 20 inches.

Old Storyteller of Taos, oil on canvas, 40 1/2 x 43 inches.

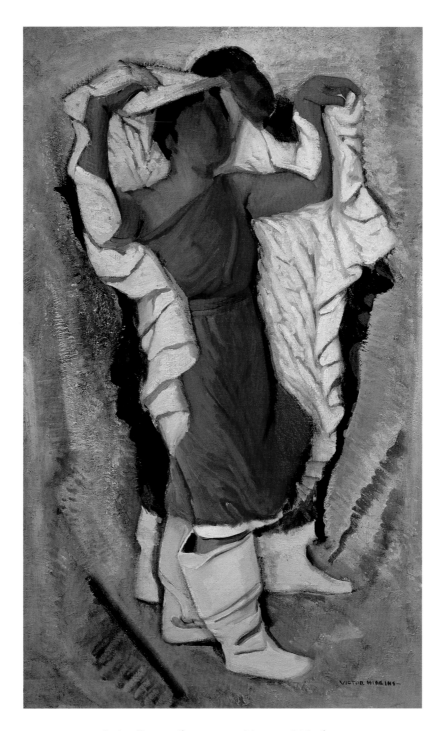

Spring Breeze, oil on canvas, 31 1/2 x 24 inches.

Aspens at Twining, oil on canvas, 34 x 36 inches.

White Horse, oil on canvas, 16 3/8 x 20 1/8 inches.

Going Home, oil on board, 24 x 27 inches.

Landscape, oil on canvas, 27 x 27 inches.

Gray Skies, oil on masonite, 12 x 17 inches.

Red Tree, oil on masonite, 12 x 17 inches.

Julius Rolshoven was an expatriate artist whose aristocratic manner stood apart from the rough-and-tumble behavior of many Taos painters. Yet his interest in conversation and artistic philosophy made him an involved participant in the Taos Society of Artists. He became an active member in 1918, at the age of sixty. Rolshoven's own style was rooted in the late nineteenth century artistic principles of allegory and classicism, and his romantic paintings of Taos Indians won critical favor among traditional circles.

Julius Rolshoven was born on October 28, 1858, in Detroit to Frederick and Maria Theresa Rolshoven. His father, a descendant from a long line of German goldsmiths, had founded one of Detroit's leading jewelry firms. Julius was an observant, sensitive child, and by his teenage years had become an accomplished pianist intent on becoming his father's apprentice in the jewelry business. Encouraged to concentrate on drawing in order to become a better engraver, Rolshoven developed an interest in art that intensified when his father took him to see the 1876 Centennial Exposition in Philadelphia. Later that year he moved to New York and enrolled at the Cooper Institute, but quickly persuaded his father to send him to Europe for more serious study. In 1877 Rolshoven entered the Royal Academy of Fine Art in Dusseldorf. The following Spring he traveled to Munich, expecting to enroll in the academy there, but found himself working instead at a nearby art colony headed by fellow American Frank Duveneck. Duveneck's fluid, spontaneous style was based on the Baroque master Franz Hals, and when he moved his studio to Italy, Rolshoven followed. In Italy, the "Duveneck boys," as they were known, studied from Titian, Veronese, and Tintoretto, and were welcomed into the artistic circles of Florence and Venice.

Rolshoven returned to Detroit in 1885, but the meager public collections and general lack of art knowledge made him long for Italy. By 1887 he was back in Florence but quickly moved to Paris, where he studied at the Académie Julian alongside E. Irving Couse, a fellow Michigan native. In Paris, Rolshoven's classical style was well received at the annual Salons, and he also participated in the Exposition Universelle of 1889, winning a coveted silver medal. Rolshoven remained in France until 1895, when he was invited to teach in London. He continued summering in Italy, however, and settled permanently in Florence in 1902. In 1905, he purchased and restored an eleventh century castle, known now as Castello del Diavolo.

Rolshoven returned to America in 1915, forced out of Italy by the onslaught of World War I. In early 1916 he decided to visit his old friend Couse in Taos, New Mexico. Rolshoven remained in Taos for the next four to five years, where he was elected an associate member of the Taos Society of Artists in 1917, and an active member the following year. Rolshoven was fascinated with the Taos Indians, and deeply admired the way in which they coexisted harmoniously with their natural surroundings. He was also a frequent participant in the Society's annual exhibitions, and was one of the more successful members in terms of sales. Although his time in Taos was productive (it was in Taos that Rolshoven painted *The Land of the Sip-o-phe*, which, at 12 x 17 feet remains one of his more ambitious paintings), Rolshoven returned to Italy around 1920, and in 1924 his status in the Taos Society was returned to that of associate.

Untitled (Indian and Horno), pastel, 13 1/2 x 10 1/2 inches.

Taos War Chief, oil on canvas, 38 1/2 x 35 inches.

Study for To the Land of Sik, pastel on paper, 9 1/2 x 9 1/4 inches.

La Bajada Hill, oil on canvas, 32 x 26 1/4 inches.

E. Martin Hennings was a quiet, peaceable man who enjoyed the solitude of Taos as well as the intellectual stimulation his Taos Society of Artists colleagues provided. Rendered with a thick yet meticulous brushstroke, his sun drenched landscapes reflect a deep connection to the region and its native population. Although he remained an academic artist throughout his career, Hennings' technique of merging figures and landscape often lends his work a flat, decorative quality. Frozen within his tapestry-like surfaces, Hennings' cowboys and Indians seem like fixed inhabitants of a timeless world.

Martin Hennings was born to German immigrants in Penns Grove, New Jersey on February 5, 1886. When he was two, his family moved to Chicago, at that time the primary metropolitan link between the east and west coasts. Hennings was drawn towards Chicago's bustling art community, centered around the Chicago Art Institute (Chicago was host to the World's Colombian Exposition in 1893, and was the only other American venue besides New York and Boston for the breakthrough Armory show of 1913). After his first visit to the Art Institute as a teenager, Hennings knew his life had been changed profoundly, and he reportedly declared: "I know what I'm going to do; I'm going to be an artist."[1]

Upon finishing high school, Hennings enrolled in the Art Institute, graduating with honors in 1904. He continued studying there until 1906, and returned briefly in 1912, disillusioned by his experiences in the commercial art world and interested in more formal study. Although he failed to win a European scholarship in the prestigious Prix de Rome competition (he finished second), he traveled to Germany and entered the Munich Academy. In Munich he kept company with fellow Americans Walter Ufer and Victor Higgins, both of whom he had known from his Art Institute days. Like Julius Rolshoven, Hennings was forced out of Europe in 1915 by World War I. With the help of authorities in Washington, D.C., he returned to Chicago, where he set up a studio and began teaching at the Chicago Academy of Fine Arts.

As Hennings' reputation grew, he attracted the patronage of some of Chicago's most respected citizens, including former mayor Carter Harrison and Oscar Mayer, the meat-packing mogul. In 1917 Harrison suggested Hennings work in Taos for a season, with the guarantee that the resulting paintings would be purchased by himself and Mayer. Although he was deeply impressed by Taos, Hennings did not settle in there immediately; he returned to Chicago that Winter, where he worked for several more years. After careful consideration of a number of different artists' colonies on the east coast, Hennings made Taos his permanent home in 1921. Already well acquainted with Ufer and Higgins, in 1924 he was elected to active membership in the Taos Society of Artists (Hennings had been nominated for membership the previous year along with Sheldon Parsons and Theodore Van Soelen, but none received the requisite two-thirds vote). Hennings remained an active member until the Society disbanded in 1927, refusing to take sides during the controversy following the 1923 resignation of Blumenschein, whom he greatly admired.

E. MARTIN HENNINGS IN HIS STUDIO

good duc

Irrigation, oil on canvas, 36 x 40 inches.

Returning to the Pueblo, oil on canvas, 25 x 30 inches.

Work Boats Docked by a Venice Canal Bridge, oil on canvas, 16 x 20 inches.

By the Stream in Taos, oil on board, 14 x 14 inches.

Indian Fishing with Horsehair, oil on canvas, 30 x 30 inches.

New Mexico Corral, oil on canvas, 25 1/4 x 30 inches.

Portrait of a Taos Indian, oil on canvas, 14 1/4 x 10 1/4 inches.

Taos Landscape with Cabin, oil on canvas, 20 x 25 inches.

The Sheepherder, oil on canvas, 40 x 40 inches.

A prolific portrait painter and art instructor for nearly sixty years, Catharine Critcher was a strong willed, independent woman who brought to the Taos Society of Artists a genuine interest in capturing the physical appearance as well the emotional state of her Indian subjects. The first and only woman inducted into the Taos Society, Critcher's election to membership in 1924 was undoubtedly intended to help boost lagging sales from the Society's annual exhibition circuit, in which not only the artists but the patrons were almost exclusively men.

Catharine Critcher was born in Westmoreland County, Virginia, on September 13, 1868 to Elizabeth and John Critcher, a wealthy couple whose aristocratic roots could be traced to the seventeenth century. Rather than attend a traditional college, Critcher persuaded her parents to send her to the Cooper Union in New York, where she acquired the basics of an academic art education before enrolling in the Corcoran School of Art in Washington D.C. Upon completing her studies in 1901, she established herself as a portrait painter of Washington society members. Despite the success she enjoyed, in 1904 Critcher left for Europe and further training at the Académie Julian in Paris. Within a year of her arrival, she founded the Cours Critcher, a course designed to help American art students adjust to the rigors of foreign study. Critcher, whose submissions were never rejected from the annual Salon, also earned honors at the Académie and served as President of the American Women Painters in Paris. Upon her return to the U.S. in 1909 she taught at the Corcoran before resigning to open the Critcher School of Painting in 1919. Three years later she and sculptor Clara Hill opened the Critcher-Hill Art School, which she ran concurrently with the Critcher School of Painting.

When Critcher first visited New Mexico in 1920, she was immediately attracted to the expressive potential of the Spanish and Indian people. While she did produce paintings of Indians posed in landscapes and astride horses, she remains best known for her portraits of the people of the Taos pueblo - several of which won her national recognition. Although Critcher never settled permanently in Taos, she spent summers there throughout the 1920s, returning to Washington in the winters to sell and exhibit her New Mexico work. In 1924 she was nominated to membership (along with Martin Hennings) in the Taos Society of Artists by Bert Phillips and Oscar Berninghaus. A letter to C. Powell Minnegrode, the director of the Corcoran, documents her happy reaction to her subsequent election: "A letter just received from Mr. Couse informs me that I have been unanimously elected to active membership in the Taos Society of Artists. Its nice to be the first and only woman in it. I am feeling very good about it."[1] Critcher's strong reputation with eastern collectors was surely a boost to the Society's declining exhibition circuit. Although her role within the Society remains somewhat unclear, she was present at at least one annual meeting (1926), and remained a member until the group disbanded in 1927.

Flowers in a Vase, oil on canvas, 20 x 16 inches.

A Taos Hoop Dancer, oil on canvas, 30 x 30 inches.

Juanita and Family, oil on canvas, 26 x 22 inches.

Indian Drummer, oil on canvas, 18 x 17 inches.

Kenneth Adams became the last and youngest member of the Taos Society of Artists in 1926, one year before the group disbanded. While the work of most of the Taos Society members was rooted in the academic principles of the late nineteenth century, Adams was deeply influenced by the proto-cubist experiments of Cézanne and the prominent American modernist, Andrew Dasburg. Adams' use of broken forms and strong, clean lines is akin to Dasburg's interest in reducing natural shapes to the geometric essentials of line, volume, and color.

Born in Topeka, Kansas on August 6, 1897, Kenneth Adams' early interest in art was prompted by illustrations from popular magazines. Convinced that Topeka was too provincial for him to receive serious instruction, Adams moved to Chicago after high school, where he enrolled in the Art Institute. After a brief stint in the Army during World War I, Adams relocated to New York in 1919 and continued his studies at the Art Students League. In New York he met Maurice Stern (Mabel Dodge's first husband), who regularly visited Taos during the summers. He also encountered the work of Andrew Dasburg at the progressive De Zayas Gallery (Maurius De Zayas was a member of Alfred Steiglitz's circle of radical artists, which also included John Marin). Adams soon enrolled in Dasburg's class at the art colony in Woodstock, New York, where he was introduced to the tenets of Cézanne and Cubism. In 1921 at Dasburg's encouragement, Adams left for Paris where he gained firsthand experience of the work of Van Gogh, Matisse, Picasso, and Braque. Shortly after his return to the United States two years later, Adams moved to Santa Fe to work with his mentor, Dasburg. Unable to secure a sufficient studio in Santa Fe, Adams continued on to Taos. Before leaving, he obtained from Dasburg a letter of introduction to Walter Ufer, who helped the younger artist obtain a space to live and work in upon his arrival.

At the invitation of Ufer, Adams joined the Taos Society of Artists during the summer of 1926. Adams was impressed with the Society's impact upon the economic growth of the region, as well as the expansion of the art colony since its formation in 1915. Adams' style, which was fully developed by the time he arrived in Taos, reflects less interest in the romantic potential of Pueblo culture than many of his Taos Society colleagues. Rather, he applied his interest in the spatial experiments of Cézanne and Dasburg to Taos subjects with results that were uniquely his own. Adams' use of clean lines and his manipulation of geometric space lends his Indian subjects a degree of monumentality, reflective of his own belief in the inherent dignity of mankind.

Although the final meeting of the Taos Society in 1927 was never officially recorded, Adams later wrote in the *New Mexican Quarterly* that ". . . a quorum of [Taos Society] members met at the home of Bert G. Phillips one night in March, 1927, and by a unanimous vote ended the existence of the Taos Society of Artists."[1]

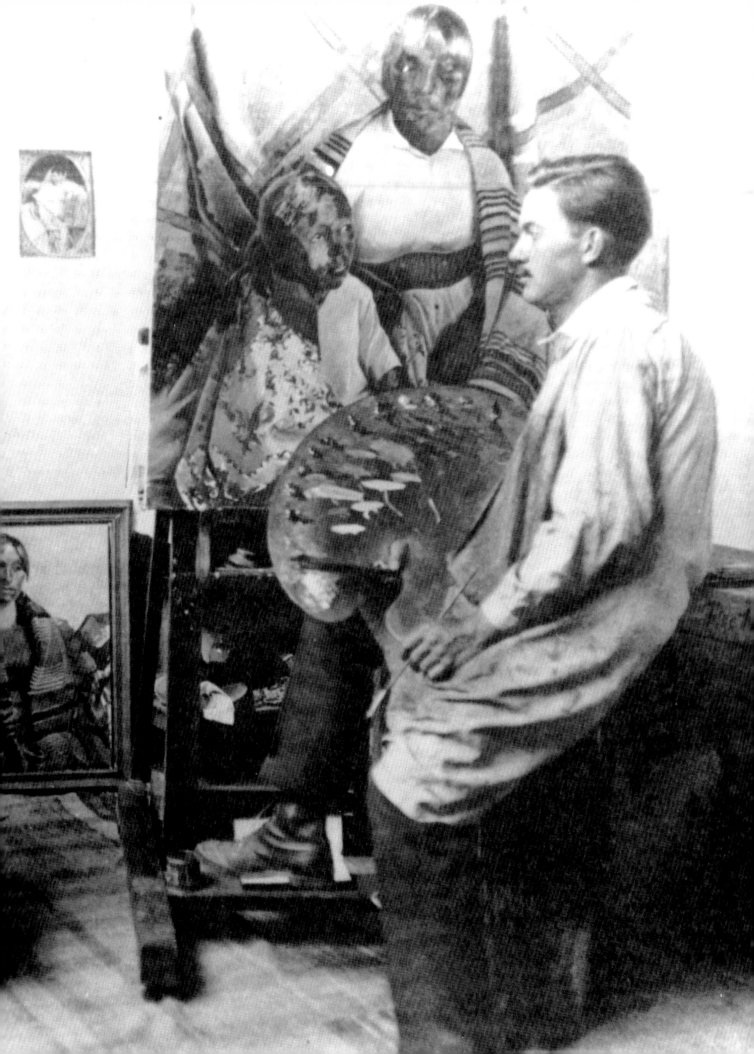

Iris, oil on canvas, 24 x 16 inches.

Taos Indian Evening, oil on canvas, 40 x 25 1/2 inches.

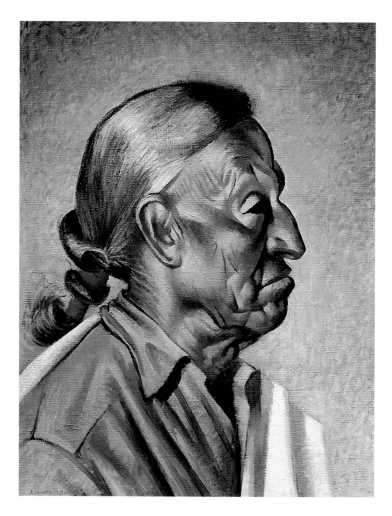

Jim Mirabal, oil on canvas, 18 x 14 inches.

The Valley, oil on canvas, 18 x 24 inches.

Gladiolas - Still Life oil on canvas, 30 x 18 inches.

New Mexico Adobes, oil on canvas, 12 x 16 1/2 inches.

Notes

Introduction

1 Blumenschein quoted in William T. Henning Jr., *Ernest Blumenschein Retrospective* (exh. cat.), Colorado Springs: Colorado Springs Fine Arts Center, 1978, p. 12.

2 Phillips quoted in Julie Schimmel, *Bert Geer Phillips and the Taos Art Colony*, Albuquerque: University of New Mexico Press, 1994, p. 65. Schimmel notes that the date and context of the quote are not known. It is from an article by Daniel McMorris for the *Kansas City Star*, reprinted in the *Santa Fe New Mexican* on November 26, 1921, p. 5.

3 Laura Bickerstaff, *Pioneer Artists of Taos*, Denver: Old West Publishing Co., 1983, p. 79. Bickerstaff notes that while Couse may have already known of Taos, the first reference connecting Couse to Taos is found in a letter from Mrs. Couse who notes that a "friend" in New York had recommended the village.

4 On at least one occasion the circuit traveled as far as Honolulu (1921). Other venues throughout the years included Boston, Philadelphia, Memphis, Dayton, Toledo, Cleveland, Wichita, Detroit, Des Moines, and Pasadena.

5 Phillips, *Secretary & Treasurer's Report, 1917*, reprinted in Robert White, ed., *The Taos Society of Artists*, Albuquerque: University of New Mexico Press, 1983, p. 26.

6 Berninghaus, *Report of the Secretary Taos Society of Artists 1920 and 21*, reprinted in White, p. 71.

7 For more information on Blumenschein's campaign and the uses of Range Finder paintings, see Robert White, "Ernest Blumenschein and the Great War," *Ayer Y Hoy en Taos*, (Winter 1986), pp. 3 - 6.

8 Berninghaus, *Special Meeting, September 27, 1918*, reprinted in White, p. 32.

9 White, in his introduction to *The Taos Society of Artists* (1983), points out that Blumenschein may have been treated wrongly during this incident. He seems to have been open to serving the following year. Furthermore, both Higgins and Phillips were excused from office in 1924 on claims of illness, with the understanding that they would serve the next year. White suggests that an angry letter Blumenschein wrote to the Society in the summer of 1922 may be among the reasons. The letter admonished the rest of the members for not recognizing his efforts as president over the previous two years, nor his wife's for accommodating the members in her home.

10 *Minutes of Meeting T.S.A., 7/12/96*, reprinted in White, p. 101.

11 Berninghaus, quoted in White, p. 13.

Bert Geer Phillips

1 Ernest L. Blumenschein, "Origin of the Taos Art Colony," *El Palacio* 20, No. 10: pp. 190-193, May 1929.

2 Bert Phillips to Ernest Blumenschein, December 14, 1898, quoted in Julie Schimmel, *Bert Geer Phillips and the Taos Art Colony*, Albuquerque: University of New Mexico Press, 1994, p. 280

Oscar E. Berninghaus

1 Berninghaus quoted in Gordon Sanders, *Oscar E. Berninghaus*, Taos Heritage Publishing Company, 1985, p. 1

William Herbert Dunton

1 Laura Bickerstaff, *Pioneer Artists of Taos*, Denver: Old West Publishing Co., 1983, p. 99.

2 Michael Grauer, in "W. Herbert 'Buck' Dunton," *Southwest Art* (July 1991) lists this date as 1914. While Dunton continued to work as an illustrator after his move to Taos, the amount of time he spent in New York versus New Mexico after the initial 1912 visit is somewhat unclear.

3 Couse, *Minutes of the Annual Meeting of the Taos Society of Artists, July 12, 1924*, reprinted in White, p. 93.

E. Martin Hennings

1 Hennings quoted in Bickerstaff, p. 195.

Catharine C. Critcher

1 Critcher to C. Powell Minnegrode, summer of 1924, quoted in Patricia Janis Broder, *Taos: A Painter's Dream*, Boston: New York Graphic Society, 1980, p. 241.

Kenneth Adams

1 White, p. 12.

The Taos Society of Artists

1877   Julius Rolshoven enrolls in the Royal Academy of Art in Düsseldorf.

1878   The Santa Fe Railroad enters New Mexico.

1881   Joseph Henry Sharp travels to Belgium and enrolls in the Antwerp Academy of Fine Arts. He remains for approximately two years before returning to Cincinnati.

1883   Sharp visits New Mexico during a trip though the American West.

1884   Eager Irving Couse moves from Saginaw, Michigan to New York City, where he enrolls in the National Academy of Design.

1886   Couse leaves for Paris, where he enters William Bougueareau's atelier at the Académie Julian.

        Sharp returns to Europe, and enrolls in the Royal Academy in Munich.

        Bert Geer Phillips enrolls in the Art Students League in New York.

1887   Sharp is at the Académie Julian, where he studies for one year.

        Rolshoven enters the Académie Julian, where he meets Couse in Bouguereau's atelier.

1890   Oscar E. Berninghaus joins the lithography firm of Compton & Sons in St. Louis.

1891   Couse leaves Paris and moves briefly to Oregon with his new wife, Virginia Leavitt.

1892   Couse returns to the Académie Julian.

        Ernest L. Blumenschein moves from Ohio to New York, where he enrolls in the Art Students League.

        Sharp marries Addie Byram, who was from a small town near Cincinnati.

1893   Sharp makes his first visit to Taos on while assignment from *Harper's Weekly*.

        Walter Ufer leaves his hometown of Lexington, Kentucky for Hamburg, Germany, where he works for a year before traveling Europe as a journeyman.

        Berninghaus accepts a job as an apprentice at the Woodward and Tiernan Printing Company, one of the largest such firms in the United States.

1894   Sharp returns to the Académie Julian.

1895   Blumenschein and Phillips are working together at the Académie Julian,
        where Sharp regales them with tales of his visit to the picturesque but remote
        village of Taos.

        Ufer enters the Royal Academy of Fine Arts in Dresden, remaining until
        1898.

1896   Couse meets Phillips, Blumenschein, and Sharp at the Académie Julian.

        Blumenschein and Phillips return to New York, where they rent a studio
        together.

1897   Sharp returns to Cincinnati from Paris.

1898   On assignment from *McClure's*, Blumenschein makes his first trip to New
        Mexico during the winter. He later returns to New York and convinces
        Phillips to travel with him from Denver to Mexico that Spring. During this
        journey, they break a wagon wheel in the rough terrain of Northern New
        Mexico. After having the wheel fixed in Taos, Phillips decides to stay on per-
        manently. Blumenschein returns to New York three months later.

        Ufer returns to Kentucky.

1899   While working for the Denver and Rio Grande Railroad, Berninghaus makes
        his first visit to Taos. He begins spending each summer there.

        Phillips marries Rose Martin, the sister of the local doctor in Taos, despite her
        family's objections.

1900   Berninghaus is taking night classes at the St. Louis School of Fine Arts. He
        marries Emelia Miller, the daughter of a local businessman.

        Ufer moves to Chicago.

1901   E. Martin Hennings enrolls in the Art Institute of Chicago.

1902   Couse makes his first visit to New Mexico, probably on the advice of
        Blumenschein. He begins summering in Taos.

        Blumenschein returns to the Académie Julian, where he studies until 1909.
        During this stay he marries fellow American Mary Shepherd Greene, an
        established Salon artist.

        Sharp moves to Crow Agency, Montana, where he spends the next several
        years chronicling the appearance of the Crow, Blackfeet, and Sioux Indians.

1903   William Herbert "Buck" Dunton moves from Montana to New York.

1904   Catharine C. Critcher enters the Académie Julian.

Hennings graduates from the Art Institute of Chicago with honors.

Ufer begins teaching at the J. Francis Smith School in Chicago.

1905   Critcher founds the Cours Critcher in Paris.

1909   Critcher accepts a teaching position at the Corcoran Art School in Washington, D.C.

The Museum of New Mexico opens in Santa Fe.

1911   Higgins travels to New York and later to Europe, where he spends several months in England before moving on to Germany.

Ufer returns to Germany for further study at the Royal Academy in Munich.

1912   Phillips, Blumenschein, Sharp, Berninghaus, Dunton, and Couse found the Taos Art Colony, an informal group banded together primarily for exhibition and sales purposes.

Higgins, Ufer, and Hennings are working together in Munich, where they are all members of the American Arts Club.

At the Art Students League in New York, Dunton hears of Taos from his instructor, Blumenschein. He moves to Taos later that year.

Sharp moves permanently to Taos.

New Mexico becomes the forty-seventh state of the Union.

1913   On August 11, *The St. Louis Republic* runs a full-page story on the growing colony of artists in Taos.

Higgins returns to Chicago.

Featuring approximately 1,300 works by leading European and American modernists, the breakthrough Armory Show opens in New York. It later travels to Chicago and Boston in a reduced format.

Emelia Berninghaus dies of diabetes.

1914   Ufer and Higgins make their first visits to Taos (separately) on the advice of former Chicago mayor Carter Harrison. Higgins settles there permanently the following year.

1915   The first annual meeting of the Taos Society of Artists takes place at the home of Dr. Martin (Phillips' brother-in-law). Berninghaus, Couse, Sharp, Dunton, and Phillips are present. Couse is elected president, Phillips is elected secretary.

Annual dues are fixed at $1.00. (Although strangely absent from this first meeting, Blumenschein is also considered a founder. It is likely that Phillips did not record the minutes from this meeting until some time afterwards, as there is no exact date given. It was most likely the 15th of July, as that was the date agreed upon for future annual meetings.)

The Taos Society of Artists holds its first major exhibition at the Palace of the Governors in Santa Fe.

Rolshoven returns to the United States, forced out of Europe by World War I.

1916   The first traveling exhibition of the Society is shown in Boulder (Colorado), Santa Fe, and Las Vegas, New Mexico. Images from the Taos Society are used extensively by the Santa Fe Railway and the Denver & Rio Grande Railway for advertisement.

Rolshoven first visits New Mexico while on his honeymoon. He stays for four or five years before returning to Florence, Italy.

1917   Ufer and Higgins are elected active members at the annual meeting. The associate membership category is established with the election of Rolshoven. A motion is carried which allows Society members to exhibit only south-western subjects in the annual exhibition circuit.

Hennings makes his first visit to Taos at the suggestion of Carter Harrison.

Berninghaus, Blumenschein, Dunton, Couse, Ufer, and Phillips are selected to paint murals in the newly built Missouri State Capitol in Jefferson City.

The Museum of Fine Arts opens in Santa Fe.

Mabel Dodge arrives in Taos.

The United States enters World War I.

1918   At the annual meeting, Rolshoven is elected an active member and Robert Henri is elected an associate member. At a special meeting on August 26, the honorary membership class is established. Edgar L. Hewett and Frank Springer are the first and only honorary members elected.

Acting as the representative for the War Service Committee of the Salmagundi Club, Blumenschein leads the members in painting "Range Finders" (large paintings of European landscapes used to train soldiers to estimate distance).

1919   At the annual meeting, the Society adopts a resolution stating that prospective members must be American citizens. Albert Groll is elected an associate member. Although he was rarely in Taos, Groll was a National Academician whose name lent prestige to the Society.

Blumenschein settles permanently in Taos.

Critcher opens the Critcher School of Painting in Washington, D.C.

Kenneth Adams moves to New York and enters the Art Students League.

Higgins marries Sara Parsons, the daughter of fellow painter Sheldon Parsons. The marriage lasts five years.

1920   Acting as president of the Society, Blumenschein calls a special meeting at his home on August 8. Three artists from Santa Fe, John Sloan, Randall Davey, and B.J.O. Nordfeldt, are invited to exhibit on the Taos Society circuit the following year.

Critcher makes her first visit to New Mexico.

Rolshoven returns to Italy.

1921   John Sloan, Randall Davey, and B.J.O. Nordfeldt are elected associate members. Blumenschein is reelected as president, Ufer as secretary and treasurer.

The Society has its first exhibition on Fifth Avenue, New York, at the Kingore Gallery. Although the exhibition received much attention from the press, there were no sales. Participants included Berninghaus, Blumenschein, Couse, Dunton, Higgins, Phillips, Sharp, Ufer, Davey, Sloan, Nordfeldt, Henri, and Groll.

Hennings establishes residency in Taos.

Kenneth Adams leaves New York for Paris.

1922   Birger Sandzen, a painter from Lindsborg, Kansas, and Gustave Baumann are elected associate members. Ufer is elected president, Berninghaus secretary and treasurer.

Dunton resigns from the Society. Blumenschein, having heard from Dunton that the secretary (Ufer), had referred to him as a "bald-headed S.B.," removes himself from the Society temporarily.

Critcher opens the Critcher-Hill School with sculptor Clara Hill.

1923   At the annual meeting, Sharp is elected president. Hennings is nominated for membership along with Theodore van Soelen and Sheldon Parsons, but none receive the requisite two-thirds vote. The Society votes to join the American Federation for the Arts.

Blumenschein writes to the Society declining the office of secretary as offered to him per the Society's constitution, citing his secretaryship in another organization (The New Mexico Painters). His unwillingness to serve becomes a heated debate among the present members, which include Ufer, Berninghaus,

Couse, Higgins, Sharp, and Phillips. Ufer, the chairman, becomes infuriated and leaves the meeting. In his stead Berninghaus calls for a vote, and the remaining members decide not to accept Blumenschein's excuse. Couse is appointed secretary, and "not having any excuse to offer took charge immediately." Blumenschein subsequently resigns from the Society.

"The New Mexico Painters" is founded by Blumenschein, Higgins, Ufer, William P. Henderson, Gustave Baumann, Jozef Bakos, Frank Applegate, and B.J.O. Nordfeldt.

1924   At the annual meeting, Hennings and Critcher are elected active members (Critcher is the first and only woman to join the Society). Dunton is nominated (again) for membership, but his name is later withdrawn after a discussion about the circumstances surrounding his previous resignation, which was most likely based on his refusal to serve as secretary. Rolshoven's status is returned to that of associate member.

Kenneth Adams moves to New Mexico to work with his mentor, Andrew Dasburg. After being unable to obtain a suitable studio, he moves to Taos later that year.

Hennings marries Helen Otte, an assistant art buyer for Marshall Field's department stores.

1925   Henri and Sloan drop out of the Society, having ignored the Society's repeated requests for dues and pictures for the annual exhibition circuit.

Berninghaus settles permanently in Taos.

1926   At the annual meeting, discussion primarily revolves around finding venues for "future exhibitions where at least one sale would be made," suggesting that the exhibition circuit was no longer an effective means of generating sales.

Adams is elected to active membership.

1927   Couse settles permanently in Taos.

The Society disbands in March, at a meeting that was not recorded.

Kenneth Adams

Oscar E. Berninghaus

Ernest L. Blumenschein

Eanger Irving Couse

Catharine C. Critcher

Joseph Henry Sharp

Walter Ufer